Top 50
AWS
Associate Architect
Interview
Questions &
Answers

Knowledge Powerhouse

DEDICATION

Dedicated
to the
Knowledge Power
in
YOU
that brings great success to your life.

Keep working hard to grow in your career and
make world a great place.

CONTENTS

ACKNOWLEDGMENTS

We thank our readers who constantly send feedback and reviews to motivate us in creating these useful books with the latest information!

INTRODUCTION

Amazon Web Services is the most popular Cloud Computing platform. There is a growing demand for Associate Architect jobs in this field.

This book contains AWS Associate Architect level interview questions that an interviewer asks. Each question is accompanied with an answer so that you can prepare for job interview in short time.

We have compiled this list after attending dozens of technical interviews in top-notch companies like- Airbnb, Netflix, Amazon etc.

Often, these questions and concepts are used in our daily work. But these are most helpful when an Interviewer is trying to test your deep knowledge of Amazon Web Services.

Once you go through them in the first pass, mark the questions that you could not answer by yourself. Then, in second pass go through only the difficult questions.

After going through this book 2-3 times, you will be well prepared to face a technical interview on AWS for an Associate Architect position.

Note: This is also reference book for our video course on AWS Interview.

https://www.udemy.com/amazon-web-services-aws-interview-preparation/?couponCode=KPOWER10

AWS Architect Interview Questions

1. What do you know about AWS Region?

An AWS Region is a completely independent entity in a geographical area. There are two or more Availability Zones in an AWS Region.

Within a region, Availability Zones are connected through low-latency links.

Since each AWS Region is isolated from another Region, it provides very high fault tolerance and stability.

Within a region, resources of a service are independent. E.g. If you create an EC2 instance in a region, it is independent of EC2 instance in another region.

For launching an EC2 instance, we have to select an AMI within the same region.

It is important to note that some AWS services like IAM do not support regions.

2. What are the important components of IAM?

The important components of Identity and Access Management (IAM) are as follows:

i. **IAM User**: An IAM User is a person or service that will interact with AWS. User can sign into AWS Management Console for performing tasks in AWS. Every User in AWS has a name and security credentials.

ii. **IAM Group**: An IAM Group is a collection of IAM users. We can specify permission to an IAM Group. This helps in managing large number of IAM users. We can simply add or remove an IAM User to an IAM Group to manage permissions for them. E.g. We can have a SysAdmin group to create users with System Admin privileges.

iii. **IAM Role**: An IAM Role is an identity to which we give permissions. A Role does not have any credentials (password or access keys). We can temporarily give an IAM Role to an IAM User to perform certain tasks in AWS.

iv. **IAM Permission:** An IAM Permission is what a user can or can not do in AWS. In IAM we can create two types of Permissions. Identity based and Resource based. We can create a Permission to access or perform an action on an AWS Resource and assign it to a User, Role or

Group. We can also create Permissions on resources like S3 bucket, Glacier vault etc and specify who has access to the resource.

v. **IAM Policy**: An IAM Policy is a document in which we list permissions to specify Actions, Resources, Effects and Conditions. This document is in JSON format. We can attach a Policy to an IAM User or Group.

3. What are the important points about AWS IAM?

Some of the important points about AWS IAM are as follows:

I.   A new User in IAM does not have any permission.

II. AWS IAM assigns an Access Key and a Secret Access Key to a new User.

III. An Access Key cannot be used to login to AWS Console.

IV. We use Access Key to access AWS via an API or Command Line interface (CLI).

V.   IAM is a universal application. It is common across all the regions in AWS.

VI. When we first setup our AWS account, we get a root account that has complete Admin access.

4. What are the important features of Amazon S3?

Some of the important features of Amazon S3 are as follows:

I. Amazon S3 provides unlimited storage for files.
II. File size in Amazon S3 can vary from 0 Bytes to 5 Terabytes.
III. The largest object (file) that can be uploaded to S3 in a single PUT request is upto 5 giga bytes.
IV. We have to store files in Buckets in Amazon S3.
V. In Amazon S3, names of buckets have to be unique globally.
VI. Amazon S3 is an Object based storage.
VII. Internally, S3 uses a key based object store. When we store an object we assign a key that is used to uniquely identify the object.

5. What is the scale of durability in Amazon S3?

Amazon S3 supports durability at the scale of 99.999999999% (11 9s)of time. This is 9 nines after decimal. It means there is a chance of losing 0.000000001% of objects being stored every year.

6. What are the Consistency levels

supported by Amazon S3?

Amazon S3 supports following consistency levels for different requests:

- PUT: Amazon S3 supports <u>Read after Write consistency</u> when we create a new object by PUT. It means as soon as we Write a new object, we can access it.
- PUT for Update: Amazon S3 supports <u>Eventual Consistency</u> when we overwrite an existing object by PUT. Eventual Consistency means that the effect of overwrite will not be immediate but will happen after some time.
- DELETE: For deletion of an object, Amazon S3 supports Eventual Consistency after DELETE.

7. What are the different tiers in Amazon S3 storage?

Different Storage tiers in Amazon S3 are as follows:

I.   **S3 Standard**: In this tier, S3 supports durable storage of files that become immediately available. This tier is used for frequent file storage and access.

II.   **S3 Standard -Infrequent Access (IA):** In this tier, S3 provides durable storage that is immediately available. But in this tier files are infrequently accessed.

III.   **S3 Reduced Redundancy Storage (RRS)**: In this tier, S3 provides the option to customers to store data at lower levels of redundancy. In this case, data is copied to multiple locations but not on as many locations as standard S3.

IV.   Glacier and DEEP_ARCHIVE:

8. How will you upload a file greater than 100 megabytes in Amazon S3?

Amazon S3 supports storing of objects or files up to 5 gigabytes in a single PUT request. To upload a file greater than 100 megabytes, we have to use Multipart upload utility from AWS. By using Multipart upload we can upload a large file in multiple parts.

Each part will be independently uploaded to S3. It doesn't matter in what order each part is uploaded.

It even supports uploading these parts in parallel to decrease overall time. Once all the parts are uploaded, this utility joins these parts as a single object or file from which the parts were created.

9. What happens to an Object when we delete it from Amazon S3?

Amazon S3 provides DELETE API to delete an object.

If we want to delete an objects from a version controlled bucket, we can specify the version of the object that we want to delete. The other versions of the Object still exist within the bucket.

If we do not specify the version, and just pass the key name, Amazon S3 will delete the object and return the version id. And the object will not appear on the bucket.

In case, Multi-factor authentication (MFA) is enabled on a bucket, the DELETE request will fail if we do not specify an MFA token.

10. What is the use of Amazon Glacier?

Amazon Glacier is an <u>extremely low cost</u> cloud based storage service provided by Amazon.

We mainly use Amazon Glacier for long-term backup

purpose.

Amazon Glacier can be used for storing data archives for months, years or even decades.

It can also be used for long term immutable storage for regulatory and archival requirements. It provides Vault Lock support for this purpose. In this option, we write once but can read the same data multiple times.

One use case is for storing certificates that can be issued once, and only original person can keep the main copy. But other users can view that copy of the certificate.

11. Can we disable versioning on a version-enabled bucket in Amazon S3?

No, we cannot disable versioning on a version-enabled bucket in Amazon S3. We can just suspend the versioning on a bucket in S3.

Once we suspend versioning, Amazon S3 will stop creating new versions of the object. It just stores the object with null version ID.

When we overwrite an existing object, it just replaces the object with null version ID. Therefore, any existing versions of the object still remain in the bucket. But there will be no more new versions of the same object except the null version ID object.

12. What are the use cases of Cross Region Replication Amazon S3?

We can use Cross Region Replication in Amazon S3 to make copies of an object across buckets in different AWS Regions. This copying takes place automatically and in an asynchronous mode.

We have to add replication configuration on our source bucket in S3 to make use of Cross Region Replication. It will create exact replicas of the objects from source bucket to destination buckets in different regions.

Some of the main use cases of Cross Region Replication are as follows:

I. **Compliance**: Sometime, there are laws/regulatory requirements that ask for storing data at farther geographic locations. This kind of compliance can be achieved by using AWS Regions that are spread across the world.

II. **Failover**: At times, we want to minimize the probability of system failure due to complete blackout in a region. We can use Cross-Region Replication in such a scenario.

III. **Latency**: In case we are serving multiple geographies, it makes sense to replicate objects in the geographical Regions that are closer to end customer. This helps in reducing the latency.

13. Can we do Cross Region replication in Amazon S3 without enabling versioning on a bucket?

No, we have to enable versioning on a bucket to perform Cross Region Replication.

14. What are the different types of actions in Object Lifecycle Management in Amazon S3?

There are mainly two types of Object Lifecycle Management actions in Amazon S3.

I. **Transition Actions**: These actions define the state when an Object transitions from one storage class to another storage class. E.g. A new object may transition to STANDARD_IA (infrequent access) class after 60 days of creation. And it can transition to GLACIER after 180 days of creation.

II. **Expiration Actions**: These actions specify what

happens when an Object expires. We can ask S3 to delete an object completely on expiration.

15. How do we get higher performance in our application by using Amazon CloudFront?

Amazon Cloud Front is a content delivery network (CDN) service that is used for delivering applications, video, data etc. If an application is content rich and is being used across multiple locations, we can use Amazon CloudFront to increase its performance. Some of the techniques used by Amazon CloudFront are as follows:

- **Caching**: Amazon CloudFront caches the copies of our application's content at locations closer to our viewers. Due to caching, our users get our content very fast. Also, caching content reduces the load on our main servers.

- **Edge/Regional Locations**: CloudFront uses a global network of Edge and Regional edge locations to cache our content. These locations cater to almost all of the geographical areas across the world.

- **Persistent Connections**: In certain scenarios, CloudFront keeps persistent connections with the main server to fetch the content quickly.

- **Other Optimizations**: Amazon CloudFront also uses other optimization techniques like TCP initial congestion window etc to deliver high performance experience.
- **Lambda@Edge**: Lambda@Edge is a feature of CloudFront service that can be used for running code closer to the users of application. This helps in making the application globally distributed and high performance.

16. What is the mechanism behind Regional Edge Cache in Amazon CloudFront?

A Regional Edge Cache location lies between the main webserver and the global edge location. When the popularity of an object/content decreases, the global edge location may take it out from the cache.

But Regional Edge location maintains a larger cache. Due to this the object/content can stay for longer time in Regional Edge location. With this optimization, CloudFront does not have to go back to main webserver to fetch the content. When it does not find an object in Global Edge location, it just looks for it in Regional Edge location.

This improves the performance of serving content to users in Amazon CloudFront.

17. What are the benefits of Streaming content?

We can get following benefits by Streaming content:

I. **Control**: We can provide more control to our users for what they want to watch. In a video streaming, users can select the locations in video where they want to start watching from.

II. **Content**: With streaming our entire content does not stay at a user's device. User receives only the part he or she is watching. Once the session is over, content is removed from the user's device.

III. **Cost**: With streaming, there is no need to download all the content to a user's device. A user can start viewing content as soon as some part is available for viewing. This saves costs since we do not have to download a large media file before starting each viewing session.

IV. **Convenience**: Streaming content provides a lot of convenience to users for interacting with the content. In case of live content, users can interact with other users who are consuming the same content. E.g. Gaming events are broadcast as streaming content.

18. What is Lambda@Edge in AWS?

In AWS, we can use Lambda@Edge utility to solve the problem of low network latency for end users.

In Lambda@Edge there is no need to provision or manage servers. We can just upload our Node.js code to AWS Lambda and create functions that will be triggered on CloudFront requests.

When a request for content is received by CloudFront edge location, the Lambda code is ready to execute.

This is a very good option for scaling up the operations in CloudFront without managing multiple servers.

19. What are the different types of events triggered by Amazon CloudFront?

Different types of events triggered by Amazon CloudFront are as follows:

I. **Viewer Request**: When an end user or a client program makes an HTTP/HTTPS request to

CloudFront, this event is triggered at the Edge Location closer to the end user.

II. **Viewer Response**: This event is triggered, when a CloudFront server is ready to respond to a request.

III. **Origin Request**: When CloudFront server does not have the requested object in its cache, the request is forwarded to Origin server. At this time this event is triggered.

IV. **Origin Response**: This event is triggered, when CloudFront server at an Edge location receives the response from Origin server.

20. What is Geo Targeting in Amazon CloudFront?

In Amazon CloudFront we can detect the country from where end users are requesting our content. This information can be passed to our Origin server by Amazon CloudFront. It is sent in a new HTTP header.

Based on different countries from which the request originates, we can generate different content for different versions of the same content. These versions can be cached at different Edge Locations that are closer to the end users of that country.

In this way, we are able to serve our end users based on their geographic locations to provide a rich user experience.

21. What are the main features of Amazon CloudFront?

Some of the main features of Amazon CloudFront are as follows:

I.	Device Detection
II.	Protocol Detection
III.	Geo Targeting
IV.	Cache Behavior
V.	Cross Origin Resource Sharing
VI.	Multiple Origin Servers
VII.	HTTP Cookies
VIII.	Query String Parameters
IX.	Custom SSL

22. What are the security mechanisms available in Amazon S3?

Amazon S3 is a very secure storage service. Some of the main security mechanisms available in Amazon S3 are as follows:

I.   **Access**: When we create a bucket or an object, only the owner gets the access to the bucket and objects.

II.   **Authentication**: Amazon S3 also supports user authentication to control who has access to a specific object or bucket.

III.   **Access Control List**: We can create Access Control Lists (ACL) to provide selective permissions to users and groups for S3 objects.

IV.   **HTTPS**: Amazon S3 also supports HTTPS protocol to securely upload and download data from cloud.

V.   **Encryption**: We can also use Server Side Encryption (SSE) in Amazon S3 to encrypt data.

23. What are the benefits of AWS Storage Gateway?

We can use AWS Storage Gateway (ASG) service to connect our local infrastructure of files etc. with Amazon cloud services for storage.

Some of the main benefits of AWS Storage Gateway are as follows:

I.   **Local Use**: We can use ASG to integrate our data in multiple Amazon Storage Services like- S3, Glacier etc with our local systems. We can continue to use our local systems seamlessly.

II.   **Performance**: ASG provides better performance by caching data in local disks. Though data stays in cloud, but the performance we get is similar to that of local storage.

III.   **Easy to use**: ASG provides a virtual machine that can be used by an easy to use interface. There is no need to install any client or to provision rack space for using ASG. These virtual machines can work in local system as well as in AWS.

IV.   **Scale**: We get the storage at a very high scale with ASG. Backend of ASG is Amazon cloud, therefore, it can handle large amounts of workloads and storage needs.

V.   **Optimized Transfer**: ASG performs many optimizations, due to which only the changes to data are transferred. This helps in minimizing the use of bandwidth.

24. What are the main use cases for AWS Storage Gateway?

AWS Storage Gateway (ASG) is a very versatile product from AWS in its usage. It solves a variety of problems at enterprise level. Some of the main use cases of ASG are as follows:

I.   **Backup systems**: We can use ASG to create backup systems. Data from local storage can be backed up into cloud services of AWS by using ASG. We can also restore the data from this backup solution on need basis. It is a replacement for Tape based backup systems.

II.   **Variable Storage**: With ASG, we can grow or shrink our Storage as per our needs. There is no need to add racks, disks etc to expand our storage systems. We can manage the fluctuations in our storage needs gracefully by using ASG.

III. **Disaster Recovery**: We can also use ASG for disaster recovery mechanism. We can create snapshots of our local volumes in Amazon EBS. In case of a local disaster, we can use our applications in cloud and recover from the snapshots created in EBS.

IV.   **Hybrid Cloud**: At times we want to use our local applications with cloud services. ASG helps in implementing Hybrid cloud solutions in which we can utilize cloud storage services with our on-premise local applications.

25. What is AWS Snowball?

AWS provides a useful service known as Snowball for transporting very large amounts of data at the scale of petabytes.

With Snowball, we can securely transfer data without any network cost.

It is a <u>physical data transfer</u> solution to store data in AWS cloud.

Once we create a Snowball job in AWS console, Amazon ships a physical storage device to our location. We can copy our data to this storage device and ship it back. Amazon services will take the Snowball device and transfer the data to Amazon S3.

It is an innovative use of physical, virtual and cloud computing technology for high volume data transfer.

26. What are Spot instances in Amazon EC2?

In Amazon EC2, we can even bid for getting a computing instance. Any instance procured by bidding is a Spot Instance.

Multiple users bid for an EC2 Instance. Once the bid price exceeds the Spot price, the user with the highest bid gets it. As long as their bid price remains higher than the Spot price, they can keep using it.

Spot price varies with supply and demand. Once Spot price exceeds Bid price, the instance will be taken back from user.

27. What is the difference between Spot Instance and On-demand Instance in Amazon EC2?

Spot Instance and On-demand Instance are very similar in nature. The main difference between these is of commitment. In Spot Instance, there is no commitment. As soon as the Bid price exceeds Spot price, a user gets the Instance. In an On-demand Instance, a user has to pay the On-demand rate specified by Amazon. Once they have bought the Instance they have to use it by paying that rate.

In Spot Instance, once the Spot price exceeds the Bid price, Amazon will shut the instance. The benefit to user is that they will not be charged for the partial hour in which Instance was taken back from them.

28. What are the different types of load balancing options provided by Amazon Elastic Load Balancing (ELB)?

Amazon Elastic Load Balancing (ELB) provides following types of load balancers:

I.   **Classic Load Balancer**: This Load Balancer uses application or network load information to route traffic. It is a simple approach of load balancing to divide load among multiple EC2 instances.

II. **Application Load Balancer**: This Load Balancer uses advanced application level information to route the traffic among multiple EC2 instances. It can even use content of the request to make routing decisions.

III. **Network Load Balancer**: The network load balancer is used for balancing the Transmission Control Protocol (TCP) or User Datagram Protocol (UDP) traffic. It can handle millions of requests per second.

29. What are the main features of Classic Load Balancer in EC2?

Some of the main features of Classic Load Balancer (CLB) in Amazon EC2 are as follows:

I. **Health Check**: Based on the result of Health Check, Classic Load Balancer can decide to route the traffic. If any instance has unhealthy results, CLB will not route the traffic to that instance.

II. **Security**: We can create security groups for CLB in Virtual Private Cloud (VPC). With these features, it is easy to implement secure load balancing within a network.

III. **High Availability**: With CLB, we can distribute traffic among EC2 instances in single or multiple Availability Zones. This helps in providing very high level of availability for the incoming traffic.

IV. **Sticky Sessions**: CLB also supports sticky session by using cookies. The sticky sessions make sure that the traffic from a user is always routed to the same instance, so that user gets seamless experience.

V. **IPv6**: CLB also supports Internet Protocol version 6.

VI. **Operational Monitoring**: We can also perform

operational monitoring in CLB and collect statistics on request count, latency etc. These metrics can be monitored in CloudWatch.

30. What are the main features of Application Load Balancer (ALB) in Amazon EC2?

Main features of Application Load Balancer (ALB) are as follows:

I. **Content-Based Routing**: In ALB, we can make use of content in the request to decide the routing of a request to a specific service.

II. **HTTP/2**: ALB supports the new version of HTTP protocol. In this protocol, we can send multiple requests on same connection. It also supports TLS and header compression.

III. **WebSockets**: ALB supports WebSockets in EC2. With WebSockets, a server can exchange real-time messages with the end-users.

IV. **Layer-7 Load Balancing**: ALB can also load balance HTTP/HTTPS application with layer-7 specific features.

V. **Delete Protection**: ALB also provides Delete

Protection option by which we can prevent it from getting deleted by mistake.

VI. **Containerized Application Support**: We can use ALB to load balance multiple containers across multiple ports on same EC2 instance.

31. What is the difference between Volume and Snapshot in Amazon Web Services?

In Amazon Web Services, a Volume is a durable, block level storage device that can be attached to a single EC2 instance. In simple words, it is like a hard disk on which we can write or read from.

A Snapshot is created by copying the data of a volume to another location at a specific time. We can even replicate same Snapshot to multiple availability zones. So Snapshot is a single point in time view of a volume.

We can create a Snapshot only when we have a Volume. Also from a Snapshot we can create a Volume.

In AWS, we have to pay for storage used by a Volume as well as the one used by Snapshots.

32. What are the two main types

of Volume provided by Amazon EBS?

Amazon EBS provides following two main types of Volume:

I. **Solid State Drive (SSD)**: This type of Volume is backed by a Solid State Drive. It is suitable for transactional work in which there are frequent reads and writes. It is generally more expensive than the HDD based volume.

II. **Hard Disk Drive (HDD)**: This type of Volume is backed by Hard Disk Drive. It is more suitable for large streaming workload in which throughput it more important than transactional work. It is a cheaper option compared to SSD Volume.

33. What is the difference between Instance Store and EBS?

Some of the Amazon EC instance types provide the option of using a directly attached block-device storage. This kind of storage is known as Instance Store. In other Amazon EC2 instances, we have to attach an Elastic Block Store (EBS).

I.   **Persistence**: The main difference between Instance Store and EBS is that in Instance Store data is not persisted for long-term use. If the Instance terminates or fails, we can lose Instance Store data.

Any data stored in EBS is persisted for longer duration. Even if an instance fails, we can use the data stored in EBS to connect it to another EC2 instance.

II. **Encryption**: EBS provides a full-volume encryption of data stored in it. Whereas, Instance Store is not considered as a good storage option for encrypted data.

34. What is an Elastic IP Address?

Amazon provides an Elastic IP Address with an AWS account. An Elastic IP address is a public and static IP address based on IPv4 protocol. It is designed for dynamic cloud computing.

This IP address is reachable from the Internet. If we do not have a specific IP address for our EC2 instance, then we can associate our instance to the Elastic IP address of our AWS account. Now our instance can communicate on the Internet with this Elastic IP Address.

35. What are the benefits of using a Virtual Private Cloud in AWS?

We can get following benefits by using Virtual Private Cloud (VPC) in an AWS account:

I. We can assign Static IPv4 addresses to our instances in VPC. These static IP addresses will persist even after restarting an instance.

II. We can use IPv6 addresses with our instances in VPC.

III. VPC also allows us to run our instances on single tenant hardware.

IV. We can define Access Control List (ACL) to add another layer of security to our instances in VPC.

V. VPC also allows for changing the security group membership of instances while they are running.

36. What is a Placement Group in EC2?

AWS provides an option of creating a Placement Group in EC2 to logically group the instances within a single Availability Zone.

We get the benefits of low network latency and high network throughput by using a Placement Group.

Placement Group is a free option as of now. When we stop an instance, it will run in same Placement Group in restart at a later point of time.

The biggest limitation of Placement Group is that we cannot add Instances from multiple availability zones to one Placement Group.

37. What are the main options available in Amazon CloudWatch?

Amazon CloudWatch is a monitoring service by Amazon for cloud based AWS resources. Some of the main options in Amazon CloudWatch are as follows:

I.   **Logs**: We can monitor and store logs generated by EC2 instances and our application in

CloudWatch. We can store the log data for time period convenient for our use.

II.   **Dashboard**: We can create visual Dashboards in the form of graphs to monitor our AWS resources in CloudWatch.

III. **Alarms**: We can set alarms in CloudWatch. These alarms can notify us by email or text when a specific metric crosses a threshold. These alarms can also detect the event when an Instance starts or shuts down.

IV.   **Events**: In CloudWatch we can also set up events that are triggered by an Alarm. These events can take an automated action when a specific Alarm is triggered.

V.   **Synthetics**: In CloudWatch, we can use Synthetics to monitor the applications 24X7. It can run tests on the endpoint every minute to ensure that application is working as expected.

38. What is a Serverless application in AWS?

In AWS, we can create applications based on AWS Lambda. These applications are composed of functions that are triggered by an event. These functions are executed by AWS in cloud. But we do not have to specify/buy any instances or server for running these functions. An application created on AWS Lambda is called Serverless application in AWS.

39. How will you manage and run a serverless application in AWS?

We can use AWS Serverless Application Model (AWS SAM) to deploy and run a serverless application. AWS SAM is not a server or software. It is just a specification that has to be followed for creating a serverless application.

Once we create our serverless application, we can use CodePipeline to release and deploy it in AWS. CodePipeline is built on Continuous Integration Continuous Deployment (CI/CD) concept.

40. What is AWS Lambda?

AWS Lambda is a service from Amazon to run a specific piece of code in Amazon cloud, without provisioning any server. So there is no effort involved in administration of servers.

In AWS Lambda, we are not charged until our code starts running. Therefore, it is a cost effective solution to execute code in cloud.

AWS Lambda can automatically scale our application when the number of requests to run the code increases. Therefore, we do not have to worry about scalability of application while using AWS Lambda.

41. What are the main use cases for AWS Lambda?

Some of the main use cases in which AWS Lambda can be used are as follows:

I.   **Web Application**: We can integrate AWS Lambda with other AWS Services to create a web application that can scale up or down with zero administrative effort for server management, backup or scalability.

II. **Internet of Things (IoT):** In the Internet of Things applications, we can use AWS Lambda to execute a piece of code on the basis of an event that is triggered by a device.

III. **Mobile Backend**: We can create Backend applications for Mobile apps by using AWS Lambda.

IV.   **Real-time Stream Processing**: We can use AWS Lambda with Amazon Kinesis for processing real-time streaming data.

V.   **ETL**: We can use AWS Lambda for Extract, Transform, and Load (ETL) operations in data warehousing applications. AWS Lambda can execute the code that can validate data, filter information, sort data or transform data from one form to another form.

VI.   **Real-time File processing**: AWS Lambda can also be used for handling any updates to a file in Amazon S3. When we upload a file to S3, AWS Lambda can create thumbnails, index files, new formats etc in real-time.

42. How does AWS Lambda handle failure during event processing?

In AWS Lambda we can run a function in synchronous or asynchronous mode.

In synchronous mode, if AWS Lambda function fails, then it will just give an exception to the calling application.

In asynchronous mode, if AWS Lambda function fails then it will retry the same function at least 3 times.

If AWS Lambda is running in response to an event in Amazon DynamoDB or Amazon Kinesis, then the event will be retried till the Lambda function succeeds or the data expires.

In DynamoDB or Kinesis, AWS maintains data for at least 24 hours.

43. What are the different routing policies available in Route 53?

Route 53 service from Amazon provides multiple options for creating a Routing policy. Some of these options are as follows:

I.   **Simple Routing**: In this option, Route 53 will respond to DNS queries based on the values in resource record set.

II. **Weighted Routing**: In this policy, we can specify the weightage according to which multiple resources will handle the load. E.g. If we have two webservers, we can divide load in 40/60 ration on these servers.

III. **Latency Routing**: In this option, Route 53 will respond to DNS queries with the resources that provide the best latency.

IV. **Failover Routing**: We can configure

active/passive failover by using this policy. One resource will get all the traffic when it is up. Once first resource is down, all the traffic will be routed to second resource that is active during failover.

V.   **Geolocation Routing**: As the name suggests, this policy works on the basis of location of end users from where requests originate.

44. What are the main benefits of using Amazon DynamoDB?

Amazon DynamoDB is a highly scalable NoSQL database that has very fast performance. Some of the main benefits of using Amazon DynamoDB are as follows:

I.   **Administration**: In Amazon DynamoDB, we do not have to spend effort on administration of database. There are no servers to provision or manage. We just create our tables and start using them.

II.   **Scalability**: DynamoDB provides the option to specify the capacity that we need for a table. Rest of the scalability is done under the hood by DynamoDB.

III.   **Fast Performance**: Even at a very high scale, DynamoDB delivers very fast performance with low latency. It will use SSD and partitioning behind the scenes to achieve the throughput that a user specifies.

IV. **Access Control**: We can integrate DynamoDB with IAM to create fine-grained access control. This can keep our data secure in DynamoDB.

V. **Flexible**: DynamoDB supports both document and key-value data structures. So it helps in providing flexibility of selecting the right architecture for our application.

VI. **Event Driven**: We can also make use of AWS Lambda with DynamoDB to perform any event driven programming. This option is very useful for ETL tasks.

45. What is the basic Data Model in Amazon DynamoDB?

The basic Data Model in Amazon DynamoDB consists of following components:

I. **Table**: In DynamoDB, a Table is collection of data items. It is similar to a table in a Relational Database. There can be infinite number of items in a Table. There has to be one Primary key in a Table.

II. **Item**: An Item in DynamoDB is made up of a primary key or composite key and a variable number of attributes. The number of attributes in an Item is not bounded by a limit. But total size of an Item can be maximum 400 kilobytes.

III. **Attribute**: In DynamoDB, we can associate an Attribute with an Item. We can set a name as well as one or more values in an Attribute. Total size of data in an Attribute is maximum 400 kilobytes.

46. What are the different APIs available in Amazon DynamoDB?

Amazon DynamoDB supports both document as well as key based NoSQL databases. Due to this APIs in DynamoDB are generic enough to serve both the types.

Some of the main APIs available in DynamoDB are as follows:

I. **CreateTable**
II. **UpdateTable**
III. **DeleteTable**

IV.   DescribeTable
V.   ListTables
VI.   PutItem
VII. GetItem
VIII. BatchWriteItem
IX.   BatchGetItem
X.   UpdateItem
XI.   DeleteItem
XII. Query
XIII. Scan

47. When should we use Amazon DynamoDB vs. Amazon S3?

Amazon DynamoDB is used for storing structured data. The data in DynamoDB is also indexed by a primary key for fast access. Reads and writes in DynamoDB have very low latency because it uses SSD.

Amazon S3 is mainly used for storing unstructured binary large objects based data. It does not have a fast index like DynamoDB. Therefore, we should use Amazon S3 for storing objects with infrequent access requirements.

Another consideration is size of the data. In DynamoDB the size of an item can be maximum 400 kilobytes. Whereas Amazon S3 supports size as large as 5 terabytes for an object.

In conclusion, DynamoDB is more suitable for storing

small objects with frequent access and S3 is ideal for storing very large objects with infrequent access.

48. What is the use of Amazon ElastiCache?

Amazon ElastiCache is mainly used for improving the performance of web applications by caching the information that is frequently accessed. ElastiCache webservice provides very fast access to the information by using in-memory caching.

Behind the scenes, ElastiCache supports open source caching platforms like-Memcached and Redis.

We do not have to manage separate caching servers with ElastiCache. We can just add critical pieces of data in ElastiCache to provide very low latency access to applications that need this data very frequently.

49. What are the use cases for Amazon Kinesis Streams?

Amazon Kinesis Streams helps in creating applications that

deal with streaming data. Kinesis streams can work with data streams up to terabytes per hour rate. Kinesis streams can handle data from thousands of sources. We can also use Kinesis to produce data for use by other Amazon services. Some of the main use cases for Amazon Kinesis Streams are as follows:

I.   **Real-time Analytics**: At times for real-time events like-Big Friday sale or a major game event, we get a large amount of data in a short period of time. Amazon Kinesis Streams can be used to perform real time analysis on this data, and make use of this analysis very quickly. Prior to Kinesis, this kind of analysis would take days and weeks. Whereas, now within a few minutes we can start using the results of this analysis.

II.   **Gaming Data**: In online applications, thousands of users play and generate a large amount of data. With Kinesis, we can use the streams of data generated by a large number of online players and use it to implement dynamic features based on the actions and behavior of players.

III.   **Log and Event Data**: We can use Amazon Kinesis to process the large amount of Log data that is generated by different devices. We can build live dashboards, alarms, triggers based on this streaming data by using Amazon Kinesis.

IV.   **Mobile Applications**: In Mobile applications,

there is wide variety of data available due to the large number of parameters like- location of mobile, type of device, time of the day etc. We can use Amazon Kinesis Streams to process the data generated by a Mobile App. The output of such processing can be used by the same Mobile App to enhance user experience in real time.

50. What is the difference between Amazon SQS and Amazon SNS?

Amazon SQS stands for Simple Queue Service. Whereas, Amazon SNS stands for Simple Notification Service.

SQS is used for implementing Messaging Queue solutions in an application. We can de-couple the applications in cloud by using SQS. Since all the messages are stored redundantly in SQS, it minimizes the chance of losing any message.

SNS is used for implementing Push notifications to a large number of users. With SNS we can deliver messages to Amazon SQS, AWS Lambda or any HTTP endpoint. Amazon SNS is widely used in sending messages to mobile devices as well. It can even send SMS messages to cell phones.

Top 50 AWS Associate Architect Interview Questions

Bonus Questions

These questions are from the latest services in Amazon Web Services. It is useful to know about these while appearing for an AWS interview.

51. What is Alexa for Business from AWS?

Alexa is a service from Amazon for supporting business operations. It is like an intelligent assistant.

Business users can get benefits like managing schedule, dialing into conference calls, remote controls etc. by Alexa.

The biggest benefit of Alexa is voice enabled features. This helps in keeping people effective by using voice as an input output interface.

Users can use shared devices like printers etc at work place by giving voice commands to them

52. What are custom skills in Alexa?

Alexa provides support for building custom skills. These skills are available for use on shared devices to users that are enrolled to use these skills.

Some of the examples of custom skills are: automation of

helpdesk ticket creation, opening of doors for guests, order food for team events from pre-authorized vendors etc.

There is a Alexa Skills Kit with APIs and directions to build custom skills.

53. What is AWS Deep Learning AMI?

Amazon provides support for Deep Learning to machine learning projects. In case we want to use an AWS EC2 instance for deep learning, we can switch to AWS Deep Learning AMIs.

AWS Deep Learning AMI has built-in support for Conda and it comes with pre-installed Python environment.

It also includes popular pip package for deep learning framework.

We can also use Jupyter notebook in conjunction with AWS Deep Learning AMI to get a visual interface.

54. What is AWS Step Functions?

Amazon provides a feature called Step Functions to coordinate multiple AWS services into serverless workflows. It can be used to build apps quickly.

We can design and run workflows by using Step Functions. These workflows can be designed visually in a diagram.

Step Functions helps in stitching together applications like Amazon SageMaker, AWS Lambda etc.

An application developed with Step Functions is easier to understand as well as easier to explain to others.

Some of the examples of workflows are Machine learning model lifecycle, business report generation and IT systems automation.

55. What is Amazon SageMaker?

Amazon SageMaker is an AWS service to build, train and deploy machine learning models. It is a managed service by Amazon.

SageMaker is mainly used by data scientists for solving machine learning problems.

It helps in developing high quality maching learning models for production usecases.

SageMaker is a highly available service. It does not have any maintenance windows or downtime.

What Next?

We have a video course on Udemy.com with 100 plus questions on AWS Technical Interview.

Enjoy our promotional coupon **KPOWER10** to get it at a special discount for a limited time.

Once you buy, the course is available for lifetime access.

Course: Amazon Web Services Interview Preparation

Link: This is also reference book for our video course on AWS Interview.

https://www.udemy.com/amazon-web-services-aws-interview-preparation/?couponCode=KPOWER10

THANKS

If you enjoyed this book, then I'd like to ask you for a favor. Would you be kind enough to leave a review for this book on Amazon.com?

It'd be greatly appreciated!

Link to book:

https://www.amazon.com/Associate-Architect-Interview-Questions-Answers-ebook/dp/B01N4KGXZC

Want to go higher in your career?

Take your career to the next level with these knowledgeable books on the latest technology areas.

- Top 50 Amazon AWS Interview Questions

- Microservices Interview Questions

- Top 50 Cloud Computing Interview Questions

- Top 1000 Java Interview Questions

- Top 100 Spring Interview Questions

- Top 100 GIT Interview Questions

- Top 50 Java 8 Latest Interview Questions

- Top 50 Unix Interview Questions

- Top 50 Java Design Pattern Interview Questions

- Top 100 Java Tricky Interview Questions

- Top 50 SQL Tricky Interview Questions

- Top 50 Hibernate Interview Questions

- Top 200 Java Technical Interview Questions

REFERENCES

https://aws.amazon.com

https://aws.amazon.com/dynamodb

https://aws.amazon.com/s3

https://aws.amazon.com/ec2

https://aws.amazon.com/lambda

Made in United States
Orlando, FL
09 May 2022

17670326R10039